90 DAYS
A FAITHFUL JOURNEY
Throughout Nature

Photography by:
Marcus Nicholas

Published by Morning Dove Press
Eastern Canada's Christian Publishing House
Nova Scotia, Canada

90 Days: A Faithful Journey Throughout Nature
Text and Images Copyright © 2023 Marcus Nicholas

All rights reserved. The use of any part of this publication reproduced, transmitted in any form or by any means, electronic, mechanical, photocopying, recording, or otherwise stored in a retrieval system, without the prior written consent of the publisher — or, in case of photocopying or other reprographic copying, a licence from the Canadian Copyright Licencing Agency— is an infringement of the copyright law.

All Scripture cited in this book comes from the New Living Translation and has received approval for this use in this publication.

Edited by Morning Dove Press
Cover Design by John Ruiz, Ruiz Creative Concepts
Layout design by Linda Lebreton, Orbit Impact Marketing

A Morning Dove Press Book
Paperback ISBN 9781998057016

Published and printed in Canada
morningdovepress.ca

This 90 Day Faith Journal

New Living Translation NLT

Presented to:

_____

By:

_____

Date:

_____/_____/_____

Preface

The question we first need answered is why would a photographer write a 90 day faith journal? The answer to that question is simple. I believe, and I hope you will agree, that God is always at work around us. He is in our relationships, personal lives and in our crisis. It is so easy to think that God is silent in our lives when we don't hear the voice, see the message or prayers seem unanswered. We come to this conclusion as a result of the business of our lives. This includes our work life, family obligations, cell-phone and social media.

We don't make time for answers, only time for our requests and desires. It would be hard to argue that a walk outdoors allows us all the opportunity to be still and see creation from an abundance vantage point. Listening to the sounds of nature, wind blowing through the trees, birds, and various wildlife, can be a calming and peaceful experience.

This book seeks to take you on that walk with God as your guide. It is a simple invitation for you to grow spiritually in your faith, your belief and grow in awareness of your actions. I took all the photographs from multiple global locations and in different seasons. The images were added not to distract but to compliment your faith journey. They were added to inspire and remind you of His grace, His love and His abundance.

God has always pursued a love relationship with His children. A relationship that is personal and real. This 90 day journal encourages you to refocus and center yourself so you can adjust your life to the plan God has for you.

It's a personal journey that requires your commitment, discipline, and trust to get close to the one who loves you the most. It requires a step-by-step journey through various areas of our lives. This 90 day journal is divided into 13 weeks, themed in areas where most of us struggle. I suggest that you create a time in your day for it. Read, Reflect and Journal your thoughts. Make your ways known to the Lord.

Contents

Preface 5

Opening Prayer 9

Faith 10

Forgiveness 26

Family 42

Fellowship 58

Friendship 74

Flesh 90

Fear 106

Fasting 122

Fitness 138

Favor 154

Focus 170

Finance 186

Freedom 202

Closing Prayer 216

Acknowledgements 217

Opening Prayer

Gracious Lord, today as I begin this 90 day faith journey, grant me the wisdom I need to guide me along the way.

Open my eyes to see You in all You created; to pause and behold Your beauty in the lilies of the field; to ponder Your generosity in every fading sunset.

Generous God open my ears to hear you in the gentle patter of raindrops, in the roar of cascading waters and in the howling storms that blow my way.

In Your awesome presence I will be still and know You are God.

Amen

What Does this Verse say to you?

"You don't have enough faith," Jesus told them. "I tell you the truth, if you had faith even as small as a mustard seed, you could say to this mountain, 'Move from here to there,' and it would move. Nothing would be impossible."

- Matthew 17:20

I want to Give Thanks!

I want to Confess!

Intercession

Personal Requests

"You don't have enough faith," Jesus told them. "I tell you the truth, if you had faith even as small as a mustard seed, you could say to this mountain, 'Move from here to there,' and it would move. Nothing would be impossible."

-Matthew 17:20

I have fought the good fight, I have finished the race, and I have remained faithful. And now the prize awaits me—the crown of righteousness, which the Lord, the righteous Judge, will give me on the day of his return. And the prize is not just for me but for all who eagerly look forward to his appearing.
—2 Timothy 4:7-8

faith

What Does this Verse say to you?

I have fought the good fight, I have finished the race, and I have remained faithful. And now the prize awaits me—
the crown of righteousness, which the Lord, the righteous Judge, will give me on the day of his return.
And the prize is not just for me but for all who eagerly look forward to his appearing.
-2 Timothy 4:7-8

I want to Give Thanks!

....
....
....
....
....
....
....
....

I want to Confess!

....
....
....
....
....
....
....
....

Intercession	Personal Requests

I have fought the good fight, I have finished the race, and I have remained faithful. And now the prize awaits me—
the crown of righteousness, which the Lord, the righteous Judge, will give me on the day of his return.
And the prize is not just for me but for all who eagerly look forward to his appearing.
- 2 Timothy 4:7-8

faith

What Does this Verse say to you?

I tell you, you can pray for anything, and if you believe that you've received it, it will be yours.
- Mark 11:24

I want to Give Thanks!

....
....
....
....
....
....
....
....

I want to Confess!

....
....
....
....
....
....
....
....

Intercession	Personal Requests

I tell you, you can pray for anything, and if you believe that you've received it, it will be yours.
- Mark 11:24

faith

What Does this Verse say to you?

So you see, faith by itself isn't enough. Unless it produces good deeds, it is dead and useless.
-James 2:17

I want to Give Thanks!

....
....
....
....
....
....
....
....

I want to Confess!

....
....
....
....
....
....
....
....

Intercession	Personal Requests
....	....
....	....
....	....
....	....
....	....
....	....
....	....
....	....
....	....

So you see, faith by itself isn't enough. Unless it produces good deeds, it is dead and useless.
-James 2:17

faith

What Does this Verse say to you?

Faith shows the reality of what we hope for; it is the evidence of things we cannot see.
- Hebrews 11:1

I want to Give Thanks!

....
....
....
....
....
....
....
....

I want to Confess!

....
....
....
....
....
....
....
....

Intercession	Personal Requests
....	....
....	....
....	....
....	....
....	....
....	....
....	....
....	....
....	....
....	....

Faith shows the reality of what we hope for; it is the evidence of things we cannot see.
- Hebrews 11:1

"What do you mean, 'If I can'?" Jesus asked. "Anything is possible if a person believes."
—Mark 9:23

faith

What Does this Verse say to you?

"What do you mean, 'If I can'?" Jesus asked. "Anything is possible if a person believes."
-Mark 9:23

I want to Give Thanks!

....
....
....
....
....
....
....
....

I want to Confess!

....
....
....
....
....
....
....
....

Intercession	Personal Requests
....	....
....	....
....	....
....	....
....	....
....	....
....	....
....	....
....	....
....	....
....	....

"What do you mean, 'If I can'?" Jesus asked. "Anything is possible if a person believes."
-Mark 9:23

What Does this Verse say to you?

He replied, "What is impossible for people is possible with God.
-Luke 18:27

I want to Give Thanks!

I want to Confess!

Intercession

Personal Requests

He replied, "What is impossible for people is possible with God.
-Luke 18:27

answered prayers

forgiveness

What Does this Verse say to you?

*But when you are praying, first forgive anyone you are holding a grudge against,
so that your Father in heaven will forgive your sins, too.*
-Mark 11:25

....
....
....
....
....

I want to Give Thanks!

....
....
....
....
....

I want to Confess!

....
....
....
....
....

Intercession	Personal Requests
....	....
....	....
....	....
....	....
....	....
....	....
....	....
....	....
....	....

*But when you are praying, first forgive anyone you are holding a grudge against,
so that your Father in heaven will forgive your sins, too.*
-Mark 11:25

forgiveness

What Does this Verse say to you?

For if you return to the Lord, your relatives and your children will be treated mercifully by their captors, and they will be able to return to this land. For the Lord your God is gracious and merciful. If you return to him, he will not continue to turn his face from you.

-2 Chronicles 30:9

I want to Give Thanks!

I want to Confess!

Intercession	Personal Requests

For if you return to the Lord, your relatives and your children will be treated mercifully by their captors, and they will be able to return to this land. For the Lord your God is gracious and merciful. If you return to him, he will not continue to turn his face from you.

-2 Chronicles 30:9

forgiveness

What Does this Verse say to you?

Instead, be kind to each other, tenderhearted, forgiving one another just as God through Christ has forgiven you.
- Ephesians 4:32

I want to Give Thanks!

I want to Confess!

Intercession

Personal Requests

Instead, be kind to each other, tenderhearted, forgiving one another just as God through Christ has forgiven you.
- Ephesians 4:32

forgiveness

What Does this Verse say to you?

Do not judge others, and you will not be judged. Do not condemn others, or it will all come back against you.
Forgive others, and you will be forgiven.
- Luke 6:37

....
....
....
....
....

I want to Give Thanks!

....
....
....
....
....

I want to Confess!

....
....
....
....
....

Intercession	Personal Requests

Do not judge others, and you will not be judged. Do not condemn others, or it will all come back against you.
Forgive others, and you will be forgiven.
- Luke 6:37

forgiveness

What Does this Verse say to you?

People who conceal their sins will not prosper, but if they confess and turn from them, they will receive mercy.
- Proverbs 28:13

....
....
....
....
....

I want to Give Thanks!

....
....
....
....
....

I want to Confess!

....
....
....
....
....

Intercession	Personal Requests
....	....
....	....
....	....
....	....
....	....
....	....
....	....
....	....
....	....
....	....

People who conceal their sins will not prosper, but if they confess and turn from them, they will receive mercy.
- Proverbs 28:13

forgiveness

What Does this Verse say to you?

All the people saw him walking and heard him praising God.
- Acts 3:9

....
....
....
....
....

I want to Give Thanks!

....
....
....
....
....

I want to Confess!

....
....
....
....
....

Intercession	Personal Requests
....	....
....	....
....	....
....	....
....	....
....	....
....	....
....	....
....	....
....	....

All the people saw him walking and heard him praising God.
- Acts 3:9

forgiveness

What Does this Verse say to you?

O Lord, you are so good, so ready to forgive, so full of unfailing love for all who ask for your help.
- Psalms 86:5

....
....
....
....
....

I want to Give Thanks!

....
....
....
....
....

I want to Confess!

....
....
....
....
....

Intercession	Personal Requests

O Lord, you are so good, so ready to forgive, so full of unfailing love for all who ask for your help.
- Psalms 86:5

answered prayers

What Does this Verse say to you?

*If someone says, "I love God," but hates a fellow believer, that person is a liar;
for if we don't love people we can see, how can we love God, whom we cannot see?*
-1 John 4:20

....
....
....
....
....

I want to Give Thanks!

....
....
....
....
....

I want to Confess!

....
....
....
....
....

Intercession   ### Personal Requests

*If someone says, "I love God," but hates a fellow believer, that person is a liar;
for if we don't love people we can see, how can we love God, whom we cannot see?*
-1 John 4:20

What Does this Verse say to you?
How wonderful and pleasant it is when brothers live together in harmony!
- Psalms 133:1

....
....
....
....
....

I want to Give Thanks!

....
....
....
....
....

I want to Confess!

....
....
....
....
....

Intercession	Personal Requests
....	....
....	....
....	....
....	....
....	....
....	....
....	....
....	....
....	....
....	....

How wonderful and pleasant it is when brothers live together in harmony!
- Psalms 133:1

What Does this Verse say to you?

Make allowance for each other's faults and forgive anyone who offends you. Remember, the Lord forgave you, so you must forgive others
- Colossians 3:13

....
....
....
....
....

I want to Give Thanks!

....
....
....
....
....

I want to Confess!

....
....
....
....
....

Intercession	Personal Requests
....	....
....	....
....	....
....	....
....	....
....	....
....	....
....	....
....	....
....	....

Make allowance for each other's faults and forgive anyone who offends you. Remember, the Lord forgave you, so you must forgive others
- Colossians 3:13

family

What Does this Verse say to you?

When I was a child, I spoke and thought and reasoned as a child. But when I grew up, I put away childish things
- 1 Corinthians 13:11

....
....
....
....
....

I want to Give Thanks!

....
....
....
....
....

I want to Confess!

....
....
....
....
....

Intercession	Personal Requests
....	....
....	....
....	....
....	....
....	....
....	....
....	....
....	....
....	....
....	....

When I was a child, I spoke and thought and reasoned as a child. But when I grew up, I put away childish things
- 1 Corinthians 13:11

What Does this Verse say to you?

Fathers do not provoke your children to anger by the way you treat them. Rather, bring them up with the discipline and instruction that comes from the Lord.
- Ephesians 6:4

I want to Give Thanks!

I want to Confess!

Intercession	Personal Requests

Fathers do not provoke your children to anger by the way you treat them. Rather, bring them up with the discipline and instruction that comes from the Lord.
- Ephesians 6:4

What Does this Verse say to you?

Honor your father and mother. Then you will live a long, full life in the land the Lord your God is giving you.
- Exodus 20:12

....
....
....
....
....

I want to Give Thanks!

....
....
....
....
....

I want to Confess!

....
....
....
....
....

Intercession	Personal Requests
....	....
....	....
....	....
....	....
....	....
....	....
....	....
....	....
....	....
....	....
....	....

Honor your father and mother. Then you will live a long, full life in the land the Lord your God is giving you.
- Exodus 20:12

What Does this Verse say to you?
Direct your children onto the right path, and when they are older, they will not leave it.
— Proverbs 22:6

....
....
....
....
....

I want to Give Thanks!

....
....
....
....
....

I want to Confess!

....
....
....
....
....

Intercession | Personal Requests

Intercession	Personal Requests
....	....
....	....
....	....
....	....
....	....
....	....
....	....
....	....
....	....

Direct your children onto the right path, and when they are older, they will not leave it.
— Proverbs 22:6

answered prayers

fellowship

What Does this Verse say to you?

And why worry about a speck in your friend's eye when you have a log in your own?
- Matthew 7:3

....
....
....
....
....

I want to Give Thanks!

....
....
....
....
....

I want to Confess!

....
....
....
....
....

Intercession	Personal Requests
....	....
....	....
....	....
....	....
....	....
....	....
....	....
....	....
....	....

And why worry about a speck in your friend's eye when you have a log in your own?
- Matthew 7:3

fellowship

What Does this Verse say to you?

Jesus replied, "'You must love the Lord your God with all your heart, all your soul, and all your mind.
This is the first and greatest commandment".
- Matthew 22:37-38

....
....
....
....
....

I want to Give Thanks!

....
....
....
....
....

I want to Confess!

....
....
....
....
....

Intercession	Personal Requests
....	....
....	....
....	....
....	....
....	....
....	....
....	....
....	....
....	....

Jesus replied, "'You must love the Lord your God with all your heart, all your soul, and all your mind.
This is the first and greatest commandment".
- Matthew 22:37-38

fellowship

What Does this Verse say to you?

You must not testify falsely against your neighbor.
- Exodus 20:16

I want to Give Thanks!

I want to Confess!

Intercession

Personal Requests

You must not testify falsely against your neighbor.
- Exodus 20:16

fellowship

What Does this Verse say to you?

For where two or three gather together as my followers, I am there among them..
- Matthew 18:20

....
....
....
....
....

I want to Give Thanks!

....
....
....
....
....

I want to Confess!

....
....
....
....
....

Intercession	Personal Requests
....	....
....	....
....	....
....	....
....	....
....	....
....	....
....	....
....	....

For where two or three gather together as my followers, I am there among them..
- Matthew 18:20

Don't look out only for your own interests, but take an interest in others, too.
—Philippians 2:4

fellowship

What Does this Verse say to you?

Don't look out only for your own interests, but take an interest in others, too.
- Philippians 2:4

....
....
....
....
....

I want to Give Thanks!

....
....
....
....
....

I want to Confess!

....
....
....
....
....

Intercession | Personal Requests

Don't look out only for your own interests, but take an interest in others, too.
- Philippians 2:4

fellowship

What Does this Verse say to you?

But if we are living in the light, as God is in the light, then we have fellowship with each other, and the blood of Jesus, his Son, cleanses us from all sin.
- 1 John 1:7

....
....
....
....
....

I want to Give Thanks!

....
....
....
....
....

I want to Confess!

....
....
....
....
....

Intercession	Personal Requests
....	....
....	....
....	....
....	....
....	....
....	....
....	....
....	....
....	....
....	....

But if we are living in the light, as God is in the light, then we have fellowship with each other, and the blood of Jesus, his Son, cleanses us from all sin.
- 1 John 1:7

fellowship

What Does this Verse say to you?

So encourage each other and build each other up, just as you are already doing.
-1 Thessalonians 5:11

I want to Give Thanks!

I want to Confess!

Intercession

Personal Requests

So encourage each other and build each other up, just as you are already doing.
-1 Thessalonians 5:11

answered prayers

What Does this Verse say to you?

Never abandon a friend— either yours or your father's. When disaster strikes, you won't have to ask your brother for assistance. It's better to go to a neighbor than to a brother who lives far away.
- Proverbs 27:10

I want to Give Thanks!

I want to Confess!

Intercession | Personal Requests

Never abandon a friend— either yours or your father's. When disaster strikes, you won't have to ask your brother for assistance. It's better to go to a neighbor than to a brother who lives far away.
- Proverbs 27:10

friendship

What Does this Verse say to you?
As iron sharpens iron, so a friend sharpens a friend
- Proverbs 27:17

....
....
....
....
....

I want to Give Thanks!

....
....
....
....
....

I want to Confess!

....
....
....
....
....

Intercession	Personal Requests

As iron sharpens iron, so a friend sharpens a friend
- Proverbs 27:17

friendship

What Does this Verse say to you?

There is no greater love than to lay down one's life for one's friends.
- John 15:13

....
....
....
....
....

I want to Give Thanks!

....
....
....
....
....

I want to Confess!

....
....
....
....
....

Intercession	Personal Requests
....	....
....	....
....	....
....	....
....	....
....	....
....	....
....	....
....	....
....	....

There is no greater love than to lay down one's life for one's friends.
- John 15:13

There are "friends" who destroy each other, but a real friend sticks closer than a brother.
-Proverbs 18:24

What Does this Verse say to you?

There are "friends" who destroy each other, but a real friend sticks closer than a brother.
- Proverbs 18:24

I want to Give Thanks!

I want to Confess!

Intercession

Personal Requests

There are "friends" who destroy each other, but a real friend sticks closer than a brother.
- Proverbs 18:24

What Does this Verse say to you?

Dear friends, let us continue to love one another, for love comes from God. Anyone who loves is a child of God and knows God.

- 1 John 4:7

I want to Give Thanks!

I want to Confess!

Intercession

Personal Requests

Dear friends, let us continue to love one another, for love comes from God. Anyone who loves is a child of God and knows God.

- 1 John 4:7

friendship

What Does this Verse say to you?

*And he has given us this command:
Those who love God must also love their fellow believers.
- 1 John 4:21*

....
....
....
....
....

I want to Give Thanks!

....
....
....
....
....

I want to Confess!

....
....
....
....
....

Intercession	Personal Requests
....	....
....	....
....	....
....	....
....	....
....	....
....	....
....	....
....	....
....	....

*And he has given us this command:
Those who love God must also love their fellow believers.
- 1 John 4:21*

friendship

What Does this Verse say to you?

A friend is always loyal, and a brother is born to help in time of need.
- Proverbs 17:17

....
....
....
....
....

I want to Give Thanks!

....
....
....
....
....

I want to Confess!

....
....
....
....
....

Intercession	Personal Requests
....	....
....	....
....	....
....	....
....	....
....	....
....	....
....	....
....	....
....	....

A friend is always loyal, and a brother is born to help in time of need.
- Proverbs 17:17

answered prayers

flesh

What Does this Verse say to you?

People who conceal their sins will not prosper,
but if they confess and turn from them, they will receive mercy.
- Proverbs 28:13

....
....
....
....
....

I want to Give Thanks!

....
....
....
....
....

I want to Confess!

....
....
....
....

Intercession | Personal Requests

People who conceal their sins will not prosper,
but if they confess and turn from them, they will receive mercy.
- Proverbs 28:13

Don't be impressed with your own wisdom. Instead, fear the Lord and turn away from evil. Then you will have healing for your body and strength for your bones.
　　　　　　　　-Proverbs 3:7-8

flesh

What Does this Verse say to you?

*Don't be impressed with your own wisdom. Instead, fear the Lord and turn away from evil.
Then you will have healing for your body and strength for your bones.*
- Proverbs 3: 7-8

....
....
....
....
....

I want to Give Thanks!

....
....
....
....
....

I want to Confess!

....
....
....
....
....

Intercession	Personal Requests
....	....
....	....
....	....
....	....
....	....
....	....
....	....
....	....
....	....

*Don't be impressed with your own wisdom. Instead, fear the Lord and turn away from evil.
Then you will have healing for your body and strength for your bones.*
- Proverbs 3: 7-8

flesh

What Does this Verse say to you?

For the world offers only a craving for physical pleasure, a craving for everything we see, and pride in our achievements and possessions. These are not from the Father but are from this world.
- 1 John 2:16

....
....
....
....
....

I want to Give Thanks!

....
....
....
....
....

I want to Confess!

....
....
....
....
....

Intercession

Personal Requests

For the world offers only a craving for physical pleasure, a craving for everything we see, and pride in our achievements and possessions. These are not from the Father but are from this world.
- 1 John 2:16

flesh

What Does this Verse say to you?
Keep watch and pray, so that you will not give in to temptation.
For the spirit is willing, but the body is weak!
- Matthew 26:41

I want to Give Thanks!

I want to Confess!

Intercession

Personal Requests

Keep watch and pray, so that you will not give in to temptation.
For the spirit is willing, but the body is weak!
- Matthew 26:41

My health may fail, and my spirit may grow weak, but God remains the strength of my heart; he is mine forever.
　　　　　　-Psalm 73:26

flesh

What Does this Verse say to you?

*My health may fail, and my spirit may grow weak,
but God remains the strength of my heart; he is mine forever.
- Psalms 73:26*

....
....
....
....
....

I want to Give Thanks!

....
....
....
....
....

I want to Confess!

....
....
....
....
....

Intercession	Personal Requests
....	....
....	....
....	....
....	....
....	....
....	....
....	....
....	....
....	....
....	....

*My health may fail, and my spirit may grow weak,
but God remains the strength of my heart; he is mine forever.
- Psalms 73:26*

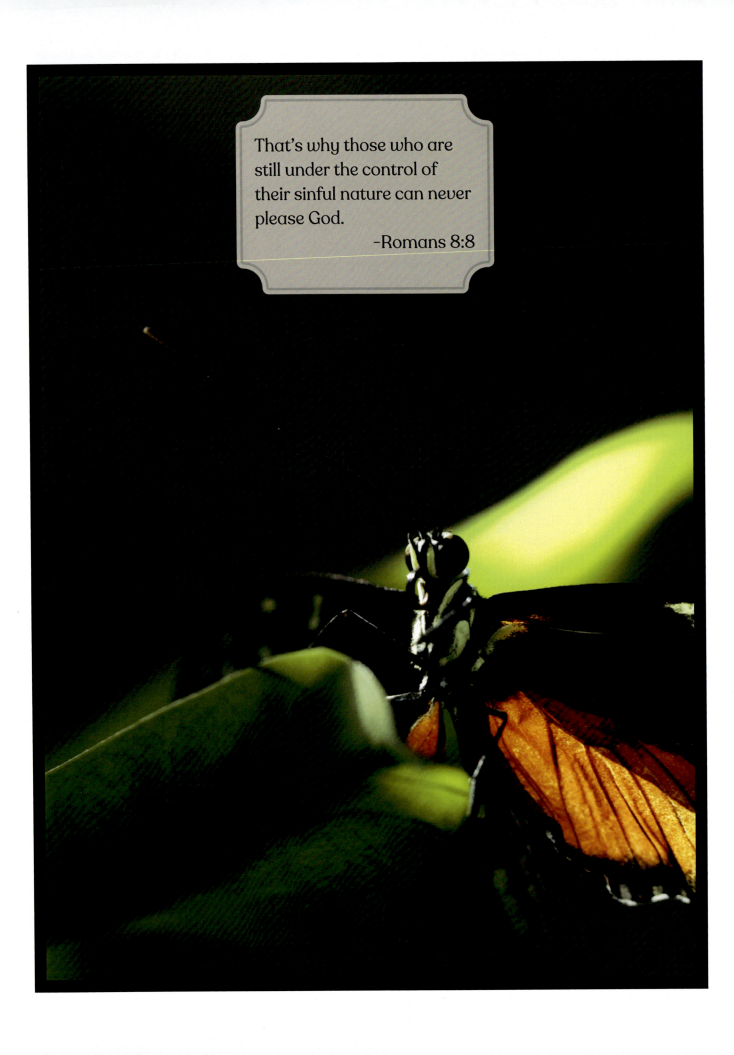

flesh

What Does this Verse say to you?

That's why those who are still under the control of their sinful nature can never please God.
- Romans 8:8

I want to Give Thanks!

I want to Confess!

Intercession

Personal Requests

That's why those who are still under the control of their sinful nature can never please God.
- Romans 8:8

So I say, let the Holy Spirit guide your lives. Then you won't be doing what your sinful nature craves.
—Galatians 5:16

flesh

What Does this Verse say to you?

So, I say, let the Holy Spirit guide your lives. Then you won't be doing what your sinful nature craves.
- Galatians 5:16

I want to Give Thanks!

I want to Confess!

Intercession

Personal Requests

So, I say, let the Holy Spirit guide your lives. Then you won't be doing what your sinful nature craves.
- Galatians 5:16

answered prayers

fear

What Does this Verse say to you?

Don't be afraid, for I am with you.
Don't be discouraged, for I am your God. I will strengthen you and help you. I will hold you up with my victorious right hand.
- Isaiah 41:10

....
....
....
....
....

I want to Give Thanks!

....
....
....
....

I want to Confess!

....
....
....
....

Intercession	Personal Requests

Don't be afraid, for I am with you.
Don't be discouraged, for I am your God. I will strengthen you and help you.
I will hold you up with my victorious right hand.
- Isaiah 41:10

fear

What Does this Verse say to you?

For God has not given us a spirit of fear and timidity, but of power, love, and self-discipline.
- 2 Timothy 1:7

....
....
....
....
....

I want to Give Thanks!

....
....
....
....
....

I want to Confess!

....
....
....
....
....

Intercession	Personal Requests

For God has not given us a spirit of fear and timidity, but of power, love, and self-discipline.
- 2 Timothy 1:7

fear

What Does this Verse say to you?

*Do not be afraid or discouraged, for the Lord will personally go ahead of you.
He will be with you; he will neither fail you nor abandon you.*
- Deuteronomy 31:8

I want to Give Thanks!

I want to Confess!

Intercession

Personal Requests

*Do not be afraid or discouraged, for the Lord will personally go ahead of you.
He will be with you; he will neither fail you nor abandon you.*
- Deuteronomy 31:8

fear

What Does this Verse say to you?
Give all your worries and cares to God, for he cares about you.
- 1 Peter 5:7

I want to Give Thanks!

I want to Confess!

Intercession

Personal Requests

Give all your worries and cares to God, for he cares about you.
- 1 Peter 5:7

fear

What Does this Verse say to you?

For I hold you by your right hand I, the Lord your God.
And I say to you," Don't be afraid, I am here to help you."
- Isaiah 41:13

....
....
....
....
....

I want to Give Thanks!

....
....
....
....
....

I want to Confess!

....
....
....
....

Intercession	Personal Requests

For I hold you by your right hand. I, the Lord your God.
And I say to you," Don't be afraid, I am here to help you."
- Isaiah 41:13

fear

What Does this Verse say to you?

This is my command: Be strong and courageous! Do not be afraid or discouraged. For the Lord your God is with you wherever you go.
- Joshua 1:9

I want to Give Thanks!

I want to Confess!

Intercession

Personal Requests

This is is my command: Be strong and courageous! Do not be afraid or discouraged. For the Lord your God is with you wherever you go.
- Joshua 1:9

fear

What Does this Verse say to you?

Such love has no fear because perfect love expels all fear. If we are afraid, it is for fear of punishment, and this shows that we have not fully experienced his perfect love.

- 1 John 4:18

I want to Give Thanks!

I want to Confess!

Intercession	Personal Requests

Such love has no fear because perfect love expels all fear.
If we are afraid, it is for fear of punishment, and this shows that we have not fully experienced his perfect love.

- 1 John 4:18

answered prayers

What Does this Verse say to you?

*When I heard this, I sat down and wept.
In fact, for days I mourned, fasted, and prayed to the God of heaven.
- Nehemiah 1:4*

....
....
....
....
....

I want to Give Thanks!

....
....
....
....
....

I want to Confess!

....
....
....
....
....

Intercession	Personal Requests
....	....
....	....
....	....
....	....
....	....
....	....
....	....
....	....
....	....
....	....

*When I heard this, I sat down and wept.
In fact, for days I mourned, fasted, and prayed to the God of heaven.
- Nehemiah 1:4*

fasting

What Does this Verse say to you?

*For the Kingdom of God is not a matter of what we eat or drink,
but of living a life of goodness and peace and joy in the Holy Spirit*
- Romans 14:17

I want to Give Thanks!

I want to Confess!

Intercession

Personal Requests

*For the Kingdom of God is not a matter of what we eat or drink,
but of living a life of goodness and peace and joy in the Holy Spirit*
- Romans 14:17

What Does this Verse say to you?

Then no one will notice that you are fasting, except your Father, who knows what you do in private.
And your Father, who sees everything, will reward you.
- Matthew 6:18

I want to Give Thanks!

I want to Confess!

Intercession

Personal Requests

Then no one will notice that you are fasting, except your Father, who knows what you do in private.
And your Father, who sees everything, will reward you.
- Matthew 6:18

What Does this Verse say to you?

So, we fasted and earnestly prayed that our God would take care of us, and he heard our prayer.
- Ezra 8:23

I want to Give Thanks!

I want to Confess!

Intercession

Personal Requests

So, we fasted and earnestly prayed that our God would take care of us, and he heard our prayer.
- Ezra 8:23

fasting

What Does this Verse say to you?

But when you pray, go away by yourself, shut the door behind you, and pray to your Father in private. Then your Father, who sees everything, will reward you.
- Matthew 6:6

I want to Give Thanks!

I want to Confess!

Intercession

Personal Requests

But when you pray, go away by yourself, shut the door behind you, and pray to your Father in private. Then your Father, who sees everything, will reward you.
- Matthew 6:6

What Does this Verse say to you?

*Don't worry about anything; instead, pray about everything.
Tell God what you need and thank him for all he has done.*
- Philippians 4: 6

....
....
....
....
....

I want to Give Thanks!

....
....
....
....
....

I want to Confess!

....
....
....
....
....

Intercession	Personal Requests

*Don't worry about anything; instead, pray about everything.
Tell God what you need and thank him for all he has done.*
- Philippians 4: 6

fasting

What Does this Verse say to you?

Be thankful in all circumstances, for this is God's will for you who belong to Christ Jesus.
— 1 Thessalonians 5:18

....
....
....
....
....

I want to Give Thanks!

....
....
....
....
....

I want to Confess!

....
....
....
....
....

Intercession	Personal Requests
....	....
....	....
....	....
....	....
....	....
....	....
....	....
....	....
....	....

Be thankful in all circumstances, for this is God's will for you who belong to Christ Jesus.
— 1 Thessalonians 5:18

answered prayers

fitness

What Does this Verse say to you?
For I can do everything through Christ, who gives me strength
- Philippians 4:13

....
....
....
....
....

I want to Give Thanks!

....
....
....
....
....

I want to Confess!

....
....
....
....
....

Intercession	Personal Requests
....	....
....	....
....	....
....	....
....	....
....	....
....	....
....	....
....	....

For I can do everything through Christ, who gives me strength
- Philippians 4:13

fitness

What Does this Verse say to you?

Don't you realize that in a race everyone runs, but only one person gets the prize?

So run to win!

- 1 Corinthians 9:24

....
....
....
....
....

I want to Give Thanks!

....
....
....
....
....

I want to Confess!

....
....
....
....
....

Intercession	Personal Requests

Don't you realize that in a race everyone runs, but only one person gets the prize?

So run to win!

- 1 Corinthians 9:24

fitness

What Does this Verse say to you?

But those who trust in the Lord will find new strength.
They will soar high on wings like eagles. They will run and not grow weary. They will walk and not faint.
- Isaiah 40:31

I want to Give Thanks!

I want to Confess!

Intercession

Personal Requests

But those who trust in the Lord will find new strength.
They will soar high on wings like eagles. They will run and not grow weary. They will walk and not faint.
- Isaiah 40:31

fitness

What Does this Verse say to you?

And you must love the Lord your God with all your heart, all your soul, all your mind, and all your strength.
- Mark 12:30

....
....
....
....
....

I want to Give Thanks!

....
....
....
....
....

I want to Confess!

....
....
....
....
....

Intercession	Personal Requests

And you must love the Lord your God with all your heart, all your soul, all your mind, and all your strength.
- Mark 12:30

fitness

What Does this Verse say to you?

Then Jesus said, "Come to me, all of you who are weary and carry heavy burdens, and I will give you rest."
- Matthew 11:28

I want to Give Thanks!

I want to Confess!

Intercession

Personal Requests

Then Jesus said, "Come to me, all of you who are weary and carry heavy burdens, and I will give you rest."
- Matthew 11:28

And so, dear brothers and sisters, I plead with you to give your bodies to God because of all he has done for you. Let them be a living and holy sacrifice—the kind he will find acceptable. This is truly the way to worship him.
—Romans 12:1

fitness

What Does this Verse say to you?

And so, dear brothers and sisters, I plead with you to give your bodies to God because of all he has done for you. Let them be a living and holy sacrifice—the kind he will find acceptable. This is truly the way to worship him.
- Romans 12:1

___

I want to Give Thanks!

___

I want to Confess!

___

Intercession	Personal Requests

And so, dear brothers and sisters, I plead with you to give your bodies to God because of all he has done for you. Let them be a living and holy sacrifice—the kind he will find acceptable. This is truly the way to worship him.
- Romans 12:1

What Does this Verse say to you?

The Lord says, "I will guide you along the best pathway for your life.
I will advise you and watch over you."
- Psalms 32:8

I want to Give Thanks!

I want to Confess!

Intercession

Personal Requests

The Lord says, "I will guide you along the best pathway for your life.
I will advise you and watch over you."
- Psalms 32:8

answered prayers

The master was full of praise. 'Well done, my good and faithful servant. You have been faithful in handling this small amount, so now I will give you many more responsibilities. Let's celebrate together

-Matthew 25:21

favour

What Does this Verse say to you?

The master was full of praise. 'Well done, my good and faithful servant.
You have been faithful in handling this small amount, so now I will give you many more responsibilities. Let's celebrate together!
- Matthew 25:21

....
....
....
....
....

I want to Give Thanks!

....
....
....
....
....

I want to Confess!

....
....
....
....
....

Intercession	Personal Requests

The master was full of praise. 'Well done, my good and faithful servant.
You have been faithful in handling this small amount, so now I will give you many more responsibilities. Let's celebrate together!
- Matthew 25:21

favour

What Does this Verse say to you?

*Wealth from get-rich-quick schemes quickly disappears;
wealth from hard work grows over time.
- Proverbs 13:11*

I want to Give Thanks!

I want to Confess!

Intercession

Personal Requests

*Wealth from get-rich-quick schemes quickly disappears;
wealth from hard work grows over time.
- Proverbs 13:11*

favour

What Does this Verse say to you?

*Commit everything you do to the Lord.
Trust him, and he will help you.
- Psalms 37:5*

....
....
....
....
....

I want to Give Thanks!

....
....
....
....
....

I want to Confess!

....
....
....
....
....

Intercession	Personal Requests

*Commit everything you do to the Lord.
Trust him, and he will help you.
- Psalms 37:5*

favour

What Does this Verse say to you?

So, you cannot become my disciple without giving up everything you own.
- Luke 14:33

....
....
....
....
....

I want to Give Thanks!

....
....
....
....
....

I want to Confess!

....
....
....
....
....

Intercession   Personal Requests

Intercession	Personal Requests
....	....
....	....
....	....
....	....
....	....
....	....
....	....
....	....

So, you cannot become my disciple without giving up everything you own.
- Luke 14:33

What Does this Verse say to you?

And it is impossible to please God without faith. Anyone who wants to come to him must believe that God exists and that he rewards those who sincerely seek him.

- Hebrews 11:6

I want to Give Thanks!

I want to Confess!

Intercession

Personal Requests

And it is impossible to please God without faith. Anyone who wants to come to him must believe that God exists and that he rewards those who sincerely seek him.

- Hebrews 11:6

favour

What Does this Verse say to you?

*So don't be afraid, little flock.
For it gives your Father great happiness to give you the Kingdom.
- Luke 12:32*

I want to Give Thanks!

I want to Confess!

Intercession | Personal Requests

*So don't be afraid, little flock.
For it gives your Father great happiness to give you the Kingdom.
- Luke 12:32*

favour

What Does this Verse say to you?

Take delight in the Lord,
and he will give you your heart's desires.
- *Psalms 37:4*

....
....
....
....
....

I want to Give Thanks!

....
....
....
....
....

I want to Confess!

....
....
....
....
....

Intercession	Personal Requests
....	....
....	....
....	....
....	....
....	....
....	....
....	....
....	....

Take delight in the Lord,
and he will give you your heart's desires.
- *Psalms 37:4*

answered prayers

What Does this Verse say to you?

Seek the Kingdom of God above all else, and live righteously, and he will give you everything you need.
- Matthew 6:33

I want to Give Thanks!

I want to Confess!

Intercession

Personal Requests

Seek the Kingdom of God above all else, and live righteously, and he will give you everything you need.
- Matthew 6:33

What Does this Verse say to you?

And now, dear brothers and sisters, one final thing. Fix your thoughts on what is true, and honorable, and right, and pure, and lovely, and admirable. Think about things that are excellent and worthy of praise.
-Philippians 4:8

I want to Give Thanks!

I want to Confess!

Intercession | Personal Requests

And now, dear brothers and sisters, one final thing. Fix your thoughts on what is true, and honorable, and right, and pure, and lovely, and admirable. Think about things that are excellent and worthy of praise.
-Philippians 4:8

What Does this Verse say to you?

But the gateway to life is very narrow and and the road is difficult, and only a few ever find it.
- Matthew 7:14

I want to Give Thanks!

I want to Confess!

Intercession

Personal Requests

But the gateway to life is very narrow and the road is difficult, and only a few ever find it.
- Matthew 7:14

> Think about the things of heaven, not the things of earth.
> —Colossians 3:2

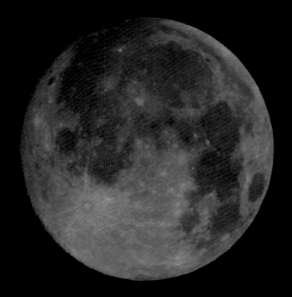

focus
What Does this Verse say to you?
Think about the things of heaven, not the things of earth.
- Colossians 3:2

I want to Give Thanks!

I want to Confess!

Intercession

Personal Requests

Think about the things of heaven, not the things of earth.
- Colossians 3:2

What Does this Verse say to you?
Look straight ahead and fix your eyes on what lies before you.
- Proverbs 4:25

I want to Give Thanks!

I want to Confess!

Intercession | Personal Requests

Look straight ahead and fix your eyes on what lies before you.
- Proverbs 4:25

focus
What Does this Verse say to you?
So don't worry about tomorrow, for tomorrow will bring its own worries. Today's trouble is enough for today.
- Matthew 6:34

I want to Give Thanks!

I want to Confess!

Intercession

Personal Requests

So don't worry about tomorrow, for tomorrow will bring its own worries.
Today's trouble is enough for today
- Matthew 6:34

What Does this Verse say to you?

*Whatever you do, do well. For when you go to the grave,
there will be no work or planning or knowledge or wisdom.*
- Ecclesiastes 9:10

....
....
....
....
....

I want to Give Thanks!

....
....
....
....
....

I want to Confess!

....
....
....
....
....

Intercession	Personal Requests

*Whatever you do, do well. For when you go to the grave,
there will be no work or planning or knowledge or wisdom.*
- Ecclesiastes 9:10

answered prayers

finances

What Does this Verse say to you?

Remember the Lord your God. He is the one who gives you power to be successful in order to fulfill the covenant he confirmed to your ancestors with an oath.

- Deuteronomy 8:18

I want to Give Thanks!

I want to Confess!

Intercession

Personal Requests

Remember the Lord your God. He is the one who gives you power to be successful in order to fulfill the covenant he confirmed to your ancestors with an oath.

- Deuteronomy 8:18

An inheritance obtained too early in life is not a blessing in the end.
—Proverbs 20:21

finances

What Does this Verse say to you?
An inheritance gained hastily at the beginning, will not be blessed at the end.
- Proverbs 20:21

I want to Give Thanks!

I want to Confess!

Intercession

Personal Requests

An inheritance gained hastily at the beginning, will not be blessed at the end.
- Proverbs 20:21

finances

What Does this Verse say to you?

No one can serve two masters. For you will hate one and love the other; you will be devoted to one and despise the other. You cannot serve God and be enslaved to money.
- Matthew 6:24

....
....
....
....
....

I want to Give Thanks!

....
....
....
....
....

I want to Confess!

....
....
....
....
....

Intercession	Personal Requests

No one can serve two masters. For you will hate one and love the other; you will be devoted to one and despise the other. You cannot serve God and be enslaved to money.
- Matthew 6:24

finances

What Does this Verse say to you?

Only ask, and I will give you the nations as your inheritance, the whole earth as your possession.
- *Psalms 2:8*

....
....
....
....
....

I want to Give Thanks!

....
....
....
....
....

I want to Confess!

....
....
....
....
....

Intercession	Personal Requests
....	....
....	....
....	....
....	....
....	....
....	....
....	....
....	....
....	....
....	....

Only ask, and I will give you the nations as your inheritance, the whole earth as your possession.
- *Psalms 2:8*

finances

What Does this Verse say to you?
Just as the rich rule the poor, so the borrower is servant to the lender.
- Proverbs 22:7

I want to Give Thanks!

I want to Confess!

Intercession

Personal Requests

Just as the rich rule the poor, so the borrower is servant to the lender.
- Proverbs 22:7

What Does this Verse say to you?

*Good people leave an inheritance to their grandchildren,
but the sinner's wealth passes to the godly.*
- Proverbs 13:22

I want to Give Thanks!

I want to Confess!

Intercession

Personal Requests

*Good people leave an inheritance to their grandchildren,
but the sinner's wealth passes to the godly.*
- Proverbs 13:22

finances

What Does this Verse say to you?

Don't store up treasures here on earth, where moths eat them and rust destroys them, and where thieves break in and steal.
— Matthew 6:19

I want to Give Thanks!

I want to Confess!

Intercession

Personal Requests

Don't store up treasures here on earth, where moths eat them and rust destroys them, and where thieves break in and steal.
— Matthew 6:19

answered prayers

If they listen and obey God, they will be blessed with prosperity throughout their lives. All their years will be pleasant.

-Job 36:11

freedom

What Does this Verse say to you?

*If they listen and obey God, they will be blessed with prosperity throughout their lives.
All their years will be pleasant.*
- Job 36:11

....
....
....
....
....

I want to Give Thanks!

....
....
....
....
....

I want to Confess!

....
....
....
....
....

Intercession	Personal Requests

*If they listen and obey God, they will be blessed with prosperity throughout their lives.
All their years will be pleasant.*
- Job 36:11

freedom

What Does this Verse say to you?
Give all your worries and cares to God, for he cares about you.
- 1 Peter 5:7

I want to Give Thanks!

I want to Confess!

Intercession

Personal Requests

Give all your worries and cares to God, for he cares about you.
- 1 Peter 5:7

What Does this Verse say to you?

Commit your actions to the Lord, and your plans will succeed.
- Proverbs 16:3

....
....
....
....
....

I want to Give Thanks!

....
....
....
....
....

I want to Confess!

....
....
....
....
....

Intercession	Personal Requests
....	....
....	....
....	....
....	....
....	....
....	....
....	....
....	....
....	....
....	....
....	....

Commit your actions to the Lord, and your plans will succeed.
- Proverbs 16:3

freedom

What Does this Verse say to you?

Then I will rejoice in the Lord. I will be glad because he rescues me.
- Psalms 35:9

....
....
....
....
....

I want to Give Thanks!

....
....
....
....
....

I want to Confess!

....
....
....
....
....

Intercession	Personal Requests
....	....
....	....
....	....
....	....
....	....
....	....
....	....
....	....

hen I will rejoice in the Lord. I will be glad because he rescues me.
- Psalms 35:9

What Does this Verse say to you?

You thrill me, Lord, with all you have done for me!
I sing for joy because of what you have done.
- Psalms 92:4

I want to Give Thanks!

I want to Confess!

Intercession

Personal Requests

You thrill me, Lord, with all you have done for me!
I sing for joy because of what you have done.
- Psalms 92:4

freedom

What Does this Verse say to you?

*Joyful is the person who finds wisdom,
the one who gains understanding.*
- Proverbs 3:13

I want to Give Thanks!

I want to Confess!

Intercession

Personal Requests

*Joyful is the person who finds wisdom,
the one who gains understanding.*
- Proverbs 3:13

answered prayers

Thank you for taking this
Faithful Journey with me.

Closing Prayer

Heavenly Father,

As I conclude this 90 day journey I pray that I continue to grow in faith and love you more. You reached out your loving arms to let me know that you will never abandon me.

I did not realize the depths you are willing to go to show me love.

During our time together, You whispered to me words of care.

You showed me your grace and mercy over my life.

I am blessed, I am thankful, for all you have done and all that you continue to do in my life and in my heart.

Please send your Holy Spirit to guide me each day to keep this commitment to spend time reading, listening, reflecting and being silent in your presence. May your will be done in me.

I ask this in the name of my Lord and Saviour Jesus Christ.

Acknowledgments

*I needed a journal like this. I could not find one.
So, I set out to write one.*

Along the way I got help.

Having an idea and turning it into a 90 day journal like this is as hard as it sounds. This being so, I would like to express my thanks to the following people who helped me to accomplish this task.

First and foremost, I wish to thank my father Martin who placed a camera in my hands at a very early age. He never offered any tips and allowed me to find my own creative path.

Any attempt at any level could not be satisfactorily completed without my godmother Lydia who always believed in me and encouraged all my endeavours. I am overwhelmed in humbleness to my uncle Barris who challenged me to always seek accurate knowledge from the bible. And always reinforced to seek first the Kingdom.

To my mother Marcella and sister Marcella-Penny who are always ready to step in and steer me in the right path in spite of their busy schedules.

To my brother-inlaw, Keith for our kayak trips and hikes which gave me the opportunity to capture a lot of images displayed in this journal.

To my aunty Bertie, thanks for all your help and guidance and providing different ideas in making this project unique.

To my children Maia and Malik, thanks for always being patient with your dad and accepting each adventure to grow.

To all the relatives and friends who helped me one way or another, I wish to say thanks to all of you for the support.

To Linda for her time and care with the layout and graphics and encouragement, I am grateful for your help.

To my partner Sea,for inspiring me to share this gift with others through the periods of self-doubt, setbacks and uncertainty, I am grateful.

*Teach me your paths
Lead me in your truth – teach it to me because you are the God who serves me.
I put my hope in You all day long.
Psalm 25, 4:5 (CEB)*